EDGE BOOKS

THE WORLD OF ARTIFICIAL INTELLIGENCE

ARTIFICIAL INTELLIGENCE
AND WORK

BY ALICIA Z. KLEPEIS

raintree
a Capstone company — publishers for children

Raintree is an imprint of Capstone Global Library Limited, a company incorporated in England and Wales having its registered office at 264 Banbury Road, Oxford, OX2 7DY – Registered company number: 6695582

www.raintree.co.uk
myorders@raintree.co.uk

Text © Capstone Global Library Limited 2020
The moral rights of the proprietor have been asserted.

All rights reserved. No part of this publication may be reproduced in any form or by any means (including photocopying or storing it in any medium by electronic means and whether or not transiently or incidentally to some other use of this publication) without the written permission of the copyright owner, except in accordance with the provisions of the Copyright, Designs and Patents Act 1988 or under the terms of a licence issued by the Copyright Licensing Agency, Barnard's Inn, 86 Fetter Lane, London, EC4A 1EN (www.cla.co.uk). Applications for the copyright owner's written permission should be addressed to the publisher.

Edited by Karen Aleo and Christopher Harbo
Designed by Brann Garvey
Original illustrations © Capstone Global Library Limited 2020
Picture research by Pam Mitsakos and Tracy Cummins
Production by Kathy McColley
Originated by Capstone Global Library Ltd
Printed and bound in India

ISBN 978 1 4747 8180 0 (hardcover)
23 22 21 20 19
10 9 8 7 6 5 4 3 2 1

ISBN 978 1 4747 7106 1 (paperback)
23 22 21 20 19
10 9 8 7 6 5 4 3 2 1

British Library Cataloguing in Publication Data
A full catalogue record for this book is available from the British Library.

Acknowledgements
We would like to thank the following for permission to reproduce photographs: Alamy: NASA Image Collection, 27, NG Images, 21, PJF Military Collection, 22-23; Getty Images: Mint/Hemant Mishra, 19, Bloomberg/David Paul Morris, 16-17, Bloomberg/ Kiyoshi Ota, 26, Denver Post/Helen H. Richardson, 25, Hero Images, 6-7; Newscom: ZUMA Press/Ringo Chiu WAI, 12, ZUMAPRESS.com/Keystone, 10; Shutterstock: Dzha33, 13, FeelGoodLuck, Cover, michaeljung, 14-15, MikeDotta, 18, Monkey Business Images, 8-9, panuwat phimpha, 11, Parilov, 24, Phonlamai Photo, 28-29, science photo, 4-5, Supphachai Salaeman, Design Element. The publisher does not endorse products whose logos may appear on objects in images in this book.

Every effort has been made to contact copyright holders of material reproduced in this book. Any omissions will be rectified in subsequent printings if notice is given to the publisher.

All the internet addresses (URLs) given in this book were valid at the time of going to press. However, due to the dynamic nature of the internet, some addresses may have changed, or sites may have changed or ceased to exist since publication. While the author and publisher regret any inconvenience this may cause readers, no responsibility for any such changes can be accepted by either the author or the publisher.

CONTENTS

INTRODUCTION
THE FUTURE OF WORK 4

CHAPTER 1
PUTTING AI TO WORK 6

CHAPTER 2
AI AND INDUSTRY................12

CHAPTER 3
AI AND DANGEROUS JOBS.......20

CHAPTER 4
PROBLEMS WITH AI 28

GLOSSARY 30
FIND OUT MORE 31
INDEX........................32

INTRODUCTION

THE FUTURE OF WORK

It's 8.00 a.m. You've just arrived at your job in a hospital **pharmacy**. The phone shows you have a message. You used to write down your voicemail messages, but not any more. An automated system changes your voice messages into text and sends them to you as emails.

After reviewing **prescriptions** on your computer, robots help you to fill them. One robot counts pills and pours them into containers. Another delivers the medications to nursing stations throughout the hospital.

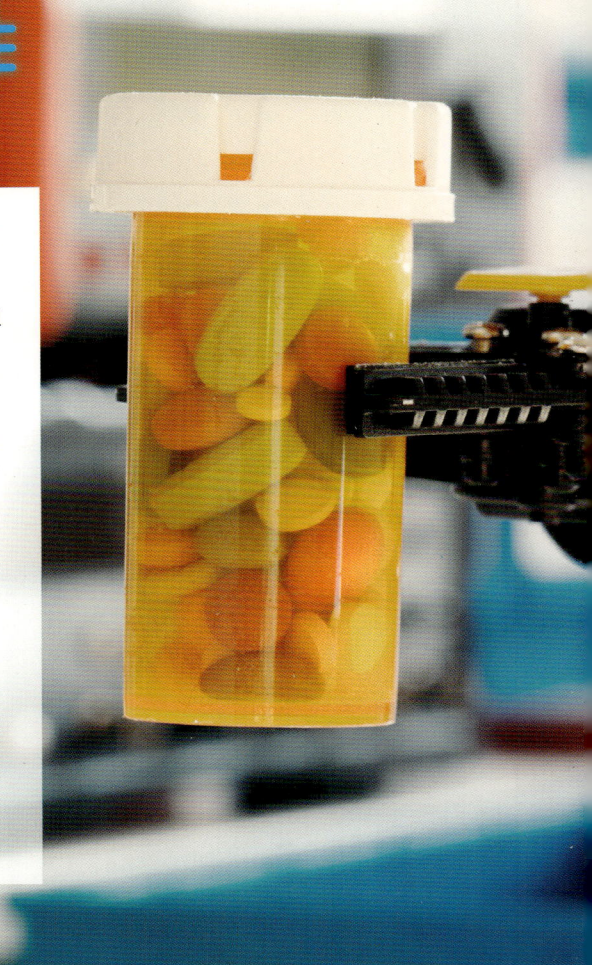

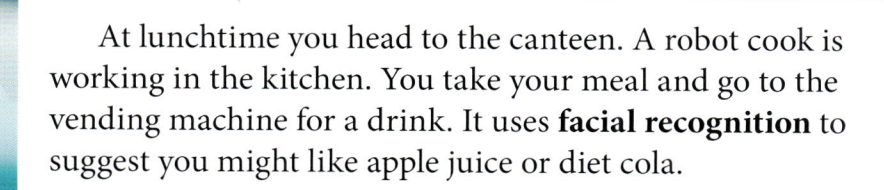

At lunchtime you head to the canteen. A robot cook is working in the kitchen. You take your meal and go to the vending machine for a drink. It uses **facial recognition** to suggest you might like apple juice or diet cola.

Does this workplace of the future sound too good to be true? It's not! With artificial intelligence (AI) the future of work is about to change.

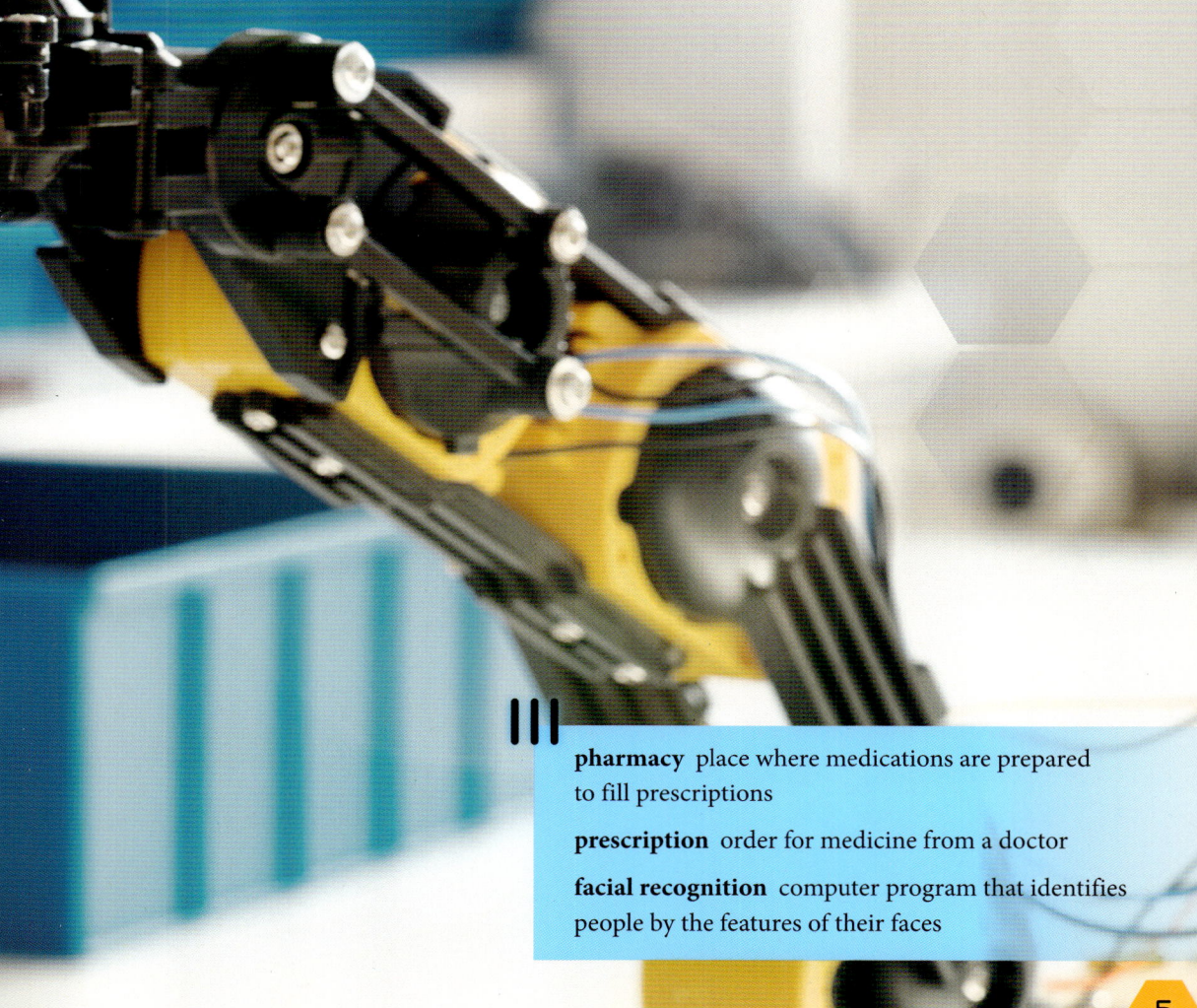

pharmacy place where medications are prepared to fill prescriptions

prescription order for medicine from a doctor

facial recognition computer program that identifies people by the features of their faces

CHAPTER 1
PUTTING AI TO WORK

What is artificial intelligence? AI allows machines to solve problems and perform tasks that normally require human intelligence. Does that mean that computers with AI can think and make decisions by themselves? Not exactly. Humans must first program computers with software that gives them clear directions.

In the world of AI, the term *algorithm* is often used. An algorithm is a detailed set of directions for solving a problem or completing a task. The set of directions for building a chair is an algorithm. So is the recipe for baking a cake. For computers and machines with AI systems, algorithms help them to perform specific tasks on their own.

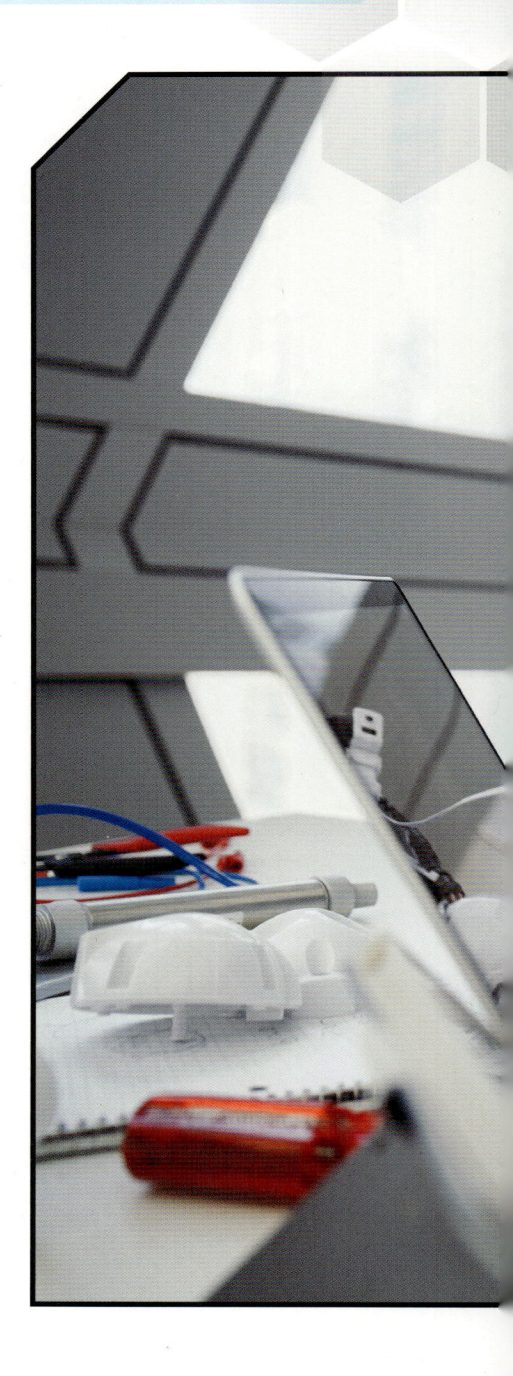

Computer programmers write the code that gives machines the ability to think and act on their own.

FACT

The term "artificial intelligence" was first used in 1956.

EARLY AI AT WORK

AI has been helping people at work for a long time. In the 1970s, AI researchers began developing programs to help doctors find the best treatment for their patients. One early program, MYCIN, helped **diagnose** blood infections by considering a patient's symptoms and medical test results. MYCIN was programmed with about 500 rules obtained from human experts.

Artificial intelligence continues to make big strides in the medical field today. Medical equipment with AI can help diagnose injuries and illnesses. Doctors can use this information to treat patients. Drug companies are starting to use AI to **analyse** different chemicals. This data helps scientists to create new medications more quickly than ever before.

A variety of medical apps use AI to help doctors diagnose and treat their patients.

diagnose find the cause of a problem

analyse examine something carefully in order to understand it

Professors attending a conference at the National Physical Laboratory in Teddington, England, test an early automatic speech recognition machine in 1958.

AI AND SPEECH RECOGNITION

The ability to speak directly to machines has long been a key goal for AI programmers. Engineers have been working on ways for machines to recognize human speech for more than 65 years. In 1952, the Automatic Digit Recognition machine was developed. Nicknamed "Audrey", this machine could recognize spoken digits from zero to nine with up to 90 per cent accuracy.

Although Audrey couldn't understand much, researchers kept working on speech recognition software. By 1971, a system called Harpy could recognize more than 1,000 words. It could even understand some sentences.

With Harpy's success, speech recognition technology took off. By the mid-1980s, IBM had created a voice-activated typewriter called Tangora. It could understand 20,000 words. By the 1990s, speech recognition had improved enough that users no longer had to speak slowly to be understood.

Today, AI and speech recognition software is very common. Many businesses use it in their customer service call centres. When customers call in, a computer system answers. It understands simple voice commands to give information, take orders or direct calls to human operators.

FACT

In 2008, a Google app brought speech recognition to mobile devices. It used the power of **cloud**-based data centres to understand what the users were saying.

cloud network of remote servers used to process, manage and store data

CHAPTER 2
AI AND INDUSTRY

Artificial intelligence is changing the way work gets done. From food service and education to manufacturing and retail, here are some ways AI is making work easier...

AI IN FOOD SERVICE

Some people think robots will one day replace fast food workers. They might be right. A CaliBurger restaurant in California, USA, has already tested a kitchen robot called Flippy. This industrial robot arm uses AI and a spatula to fry hamburgers. Using heat vision, Flippy can tell if a burger is raw or well done. Its display screen also shows human co-workers when a burger is ready for a bun.

Flippy can cook up to 2,000 burgers a day.

PIZZA DELIVERY ROBOTS

Pizzas are usually delivered by a person driving a car or a scooter. But did you know Domino's has pizza delivery robots? The company is already using them in Hamburg, Germany. The six-wheeled robots can zip around people and other obstacles in their path. They can also travel up to 16 kilometres (10 miles) per hour and work out the shortest route to their destination.

Many companies are also developing robots to make salads, pizzas and coffee. In fact, Cafe X in California, USA, has designed a robot coffee server. It uses an industrial robot arm to make and serve up to 120 coffee drinks an hour.

EDUCATION AND THE NEWS

AI isn't only used to serve food. It's also useful for serving up information in the classroom and newsroom.

In 2016, Jill Watson was a teaching assistant for an online class at Georgia Tech in the United States. During the university term, Jill answered thousands of student questions online. But Jill wasn't human. She was a virtual teaching assistant that the professor had programmed to answer their questions. Jill answered questions with a 97 per cent accuracy rate. Most of the students had no idea she was really an AI computer program.

AI is also used to report the news. News bots such as Heliograf and BuzzBot write articles for newspapers and magazines. And Quakebot is an AI program that reports earthquake information for the *Los Angeles Times*. How do these AI reporting systems work? They collect current news information and put it into article **templates**. By using robo-reporting on simple news stories, journalists have more time to work on the complicated ones.

template document that you can use as a guide when creating one of your own

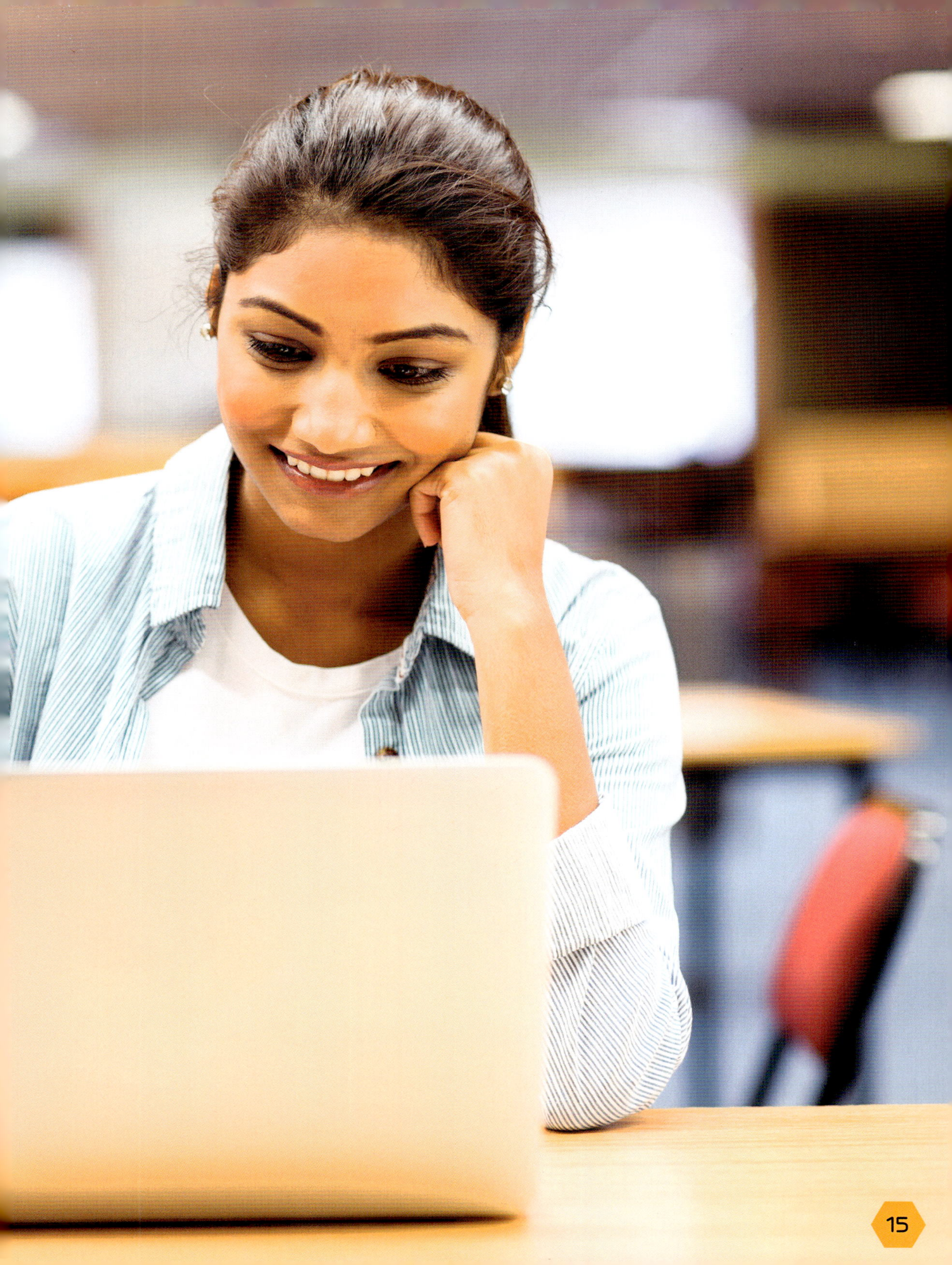

AI IN MANUFACTURING

Companies are also starting to use artificial intelligence in their factories. AI technology can reduce labour costs, cut down on product defects and speed up production. AI can even make working conditions safer.

For instance, industrial robots have been used on assembly lines for years. These robots are fast and precise. But they usually aren't intelligent enough to know they can hurt human workers. A company called KUKA is trying to change that. It has built a robot arm with special **sensors**. With the help of AI, the robot arm can work next to people without the risk of hitting or crushing them.

AI is also being used by GE, a company that makes home appliances and other equipment. In 2015, the company launched the Brilliant Manufacturing Suite. This AI system tracks every step of the manufacturing process in its factories. Sensors monitor every piece of equipment used to make various products. The AI system makes sure the whole factory runs as efficiently as possible.

FACT

AI technology can **predict** and even prevent painting defects in car manufacturing plants.

ROBOT MUSCLE

Many factories and warehouses use **autonomous** robots to carry objects from one location to another. For instance, the online retailer Amazon uses more than 100,000 robots in its warehouses around the world. Many of them are small orange robots that carry storage shelves. As orders come in, the bots bring the shelves to human workers who pick out the ordered items.

sensor instrument that detects physical changes in the environment

predict say what you think will happen in the future

autonomous able to carry out a job on one's own

Pepper is always happy to help people and answer their questions.

AI IN RETAIL

AI is creeping into the retail industry as well. In Japan, a **humanoid** robot called Pepper greets people as they enter Nescafé stores. Pepper helps sell coffee machines by answering questions and responding to people's facial expressions. The robot can even take selfies with customers.

humanoid shaped somewhat like a human

But AI in retail involves more than just robots. Have you ever looked for products on Amazon? If so, you'll probably have noticed that the site offers suggestions for products you might like each time you visit. AI technology makes these recommendations based on your recent searches and purchases.

FACT

A virtual mirror can now allow you to "try on" clothing without taking off what you're wearing. It uses AI to give you an idea of how clothes will look and fit.

CHAPTER 3
AI AND DANGEROUS JOBS

Artificial intelligence is at work in a lot of industries, but did you know it can help save lives too? After natural disasters, AI can pinpoint areas that need help from first responders. Robots and other AI devices can also handle situations that could put people in danger.

FIREFIGHTING AND RESCUE BOTS

Firefighters put their lives at risk every day. From blinding smoke and flames to hidden hazardous materials, firefighters face a host of dangers. But NASA's Jet Propulsion Laboratory has developed an AI system called AUDREY to keep them safer. AUDREY uses AI to track firefighters in smoke-filled buildings and guide them out safely. It can also identify hazardous materials and improve communication between team members.

AI even helps rescue workers find people trapped in collapsed buildings. A device called FINDER uses **radar** and algorithms to detect small motions such as heartbeats and breathing. The system is so sensitive it can pick up heartbeats through 9 metres (30 feet) of rubble.

radar device that uses radio waves to track the location of objects

Rescue workers use FINDER during a demonstration to show how its AI locates people trapped in disaster wreckage.

FACT

AUDREY stands for Assistant for Understanding Data through Reasoning, Extraction and sYnthesis. FINDER stands for Finding Individuals for Disaster and Emergency Response.

BOMB DISPOSAL ROBOTS

Disabling bombs is extremely dangerous work. Luckily, robots have been helping make bomb disposal safer for more than 40 years. But the robots don't usually work on their own. People control them from a safe distance by remote control.

However, the US military is researching ways that artificial intelligence might improve bomb disposal robots in the future. They hope AI will allow robots to spot disguised explosive devices and map dangerous locations. Future robots may even be able to feel their environment to understand the shape and texture of explosives.

FACT

Bomb disposal robots may one day work in teams. One will detect explosive devices. The other will disable them safely.

C-TURTLE, THE DISPOSABLE ROBOT

Researchers at Arizona State University, USA, have created a disposable robot that may one day locate land mines. Known as C-Turtle, this robot is made of cardboard, wires and electronics that only cost about £50. With the help of AI, it learns how to walk across different types of ground as it shuffles along like a sea turtle.

A remote-controlled bomb disposal robot approaches a large container during a training exercise.

disable stop

Drones with AI may one day help predict when problems are about to occur in large crowds.

DRONES

Have you ever seen a **drone** flying overhead? People guide these unmanned aircraft by remote control. But new ways of pairing AI with drones are taking these vehicles to new heights.

The US military is exploring the use of AI with drones as part of Project Maven. This project uses artificial intelligence to analyse large amounts of video footage taken by military drones. The AI can pick out objects of interest on the ground and flag them for human analysts to review.

While drones with AI can help to keep soldiers safer, they may help keep large crowds safe too. Researchers in the UK and India are testing drones and AI to spot violent behaviour in groups of people. The drones send video footage of large crowds to a computer AI program. The program can spot punching, kicking and other violent actions. With this system, police officers may one day be able spot and stop crime at large events and in busy public places.

FACT

The company Skycatch uses drones with AI to manage building sites. Their drones can map the work zone and work out the best way to move large equipment.

drone remote-controlled aircraft or missile that does not have an on-board pilot

ROBOTS IN SPACE

Travelling into outer space can be dangerous for humans. But unlike humans, robots don't need food or air, and they can work in the harshest of conditions. With the help of artificial intelligence, these mechanical space explorers are smarter than ever.

For years NASA has tested AI in humanoid robots. Robonaut 2 arrived at the International Space Station in 2011. With nimble hands, it helped astronauts with routine tasks. Since then, NASA has developed the more advanced Valkyrie robot. Its "brain" is made of two computers that combine input from various sensors. Scientists hope that Valkyrie might one day help humans to colonize Mars.

NASA is also including AI in the Mars 2020 rover. When this rover explores Mars in 2020, it will use AI to drive itself. AI will also help the rover to conduct science experiments and schedule its tasks based on changing conditions.

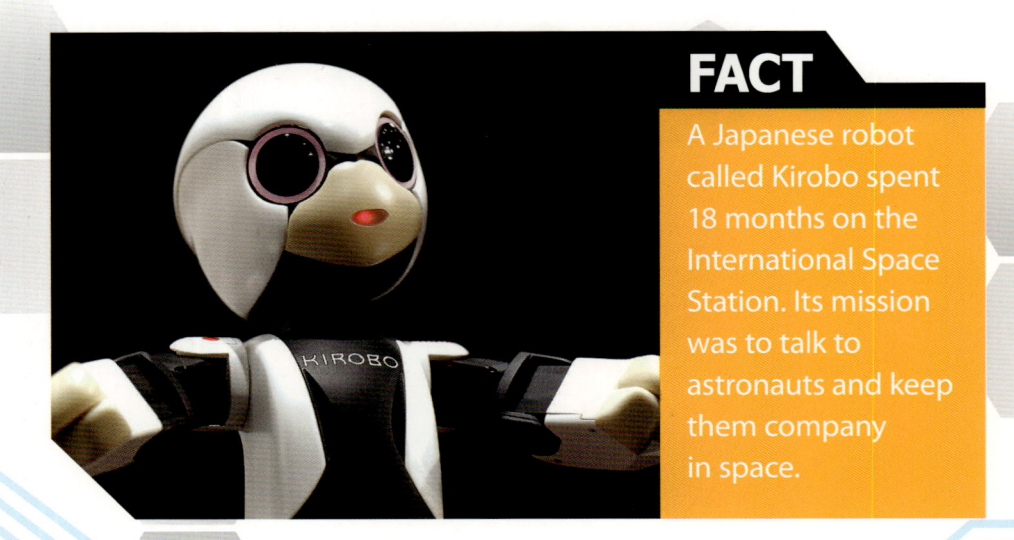

FACT

A Japanese robot called Kirobo spent 18 months on the International Space Station. Its mission was to talk to astronauts and keep them company in space.

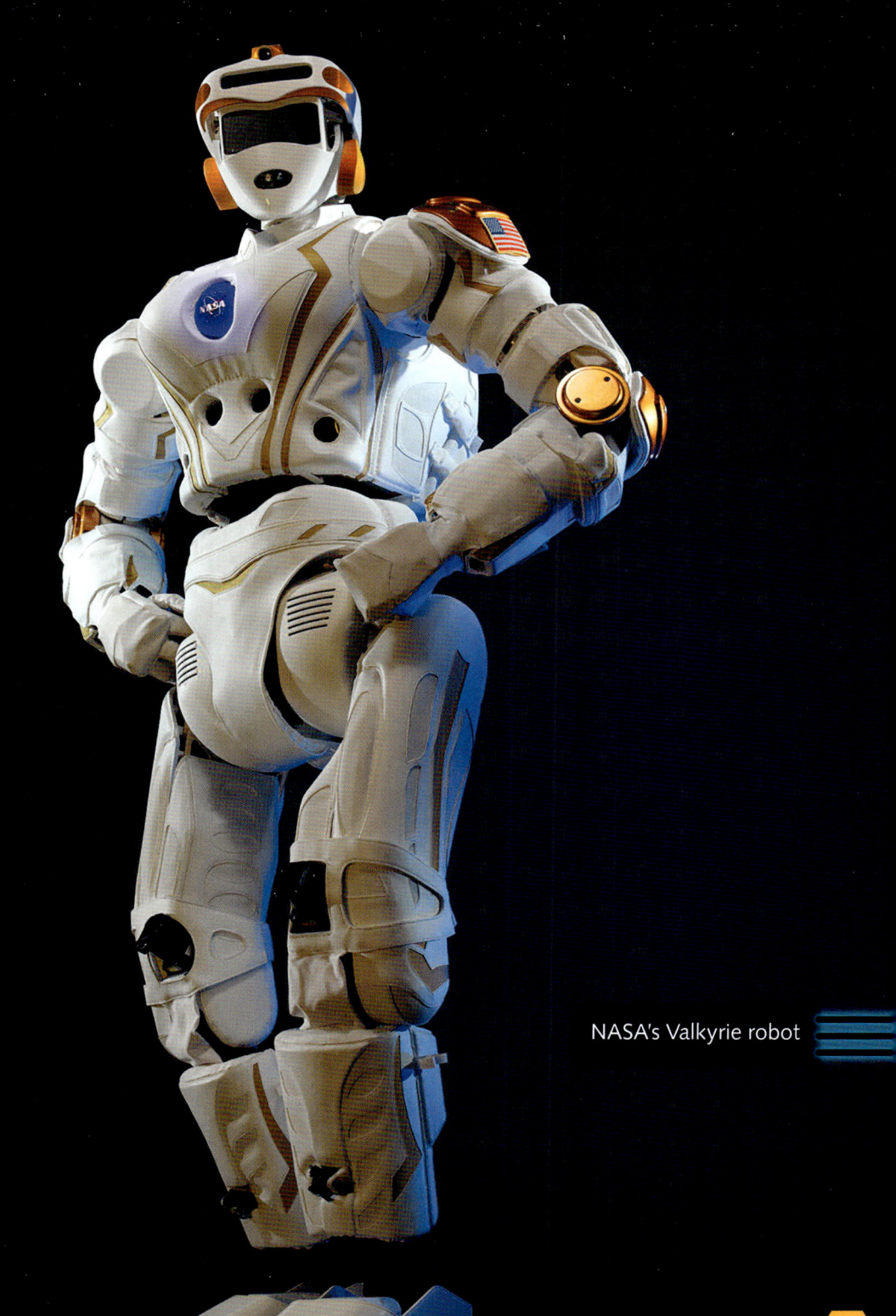

NASA's Valkyrie robot

CHAPTER 4
PROBLEMS WITH AI

From food preparation to space exploration, artificial intelligence helps people to get work done. But for all of the amazing things AI can do, are there any downsides to this technology?

Some people fear that AI will cost workers their jobs. And in some cases, it might. Especially with work that is dirty, dangerous or just plain dull. However, for every job a machine takes, the chances are that another job in a different field could be created. Many of these new jobs may be in robotics engineering or computer programming.

Other people are concerned about **bias** with AI. When AI systems are created using machine learning, any bias in the training data will show up in the AI system's behaviour. For example, if you train a speech recognition system with only male voices, women will struggle to get the system to understand them. As a result, it will appear that the system is biased towards men.

One thing is clear – the more intelligent our machines become, the more intelligent we'll need to be about the way we use them. In the meantime, the world of AI and work is changing every day. It will be exciting to see where it leads us next!

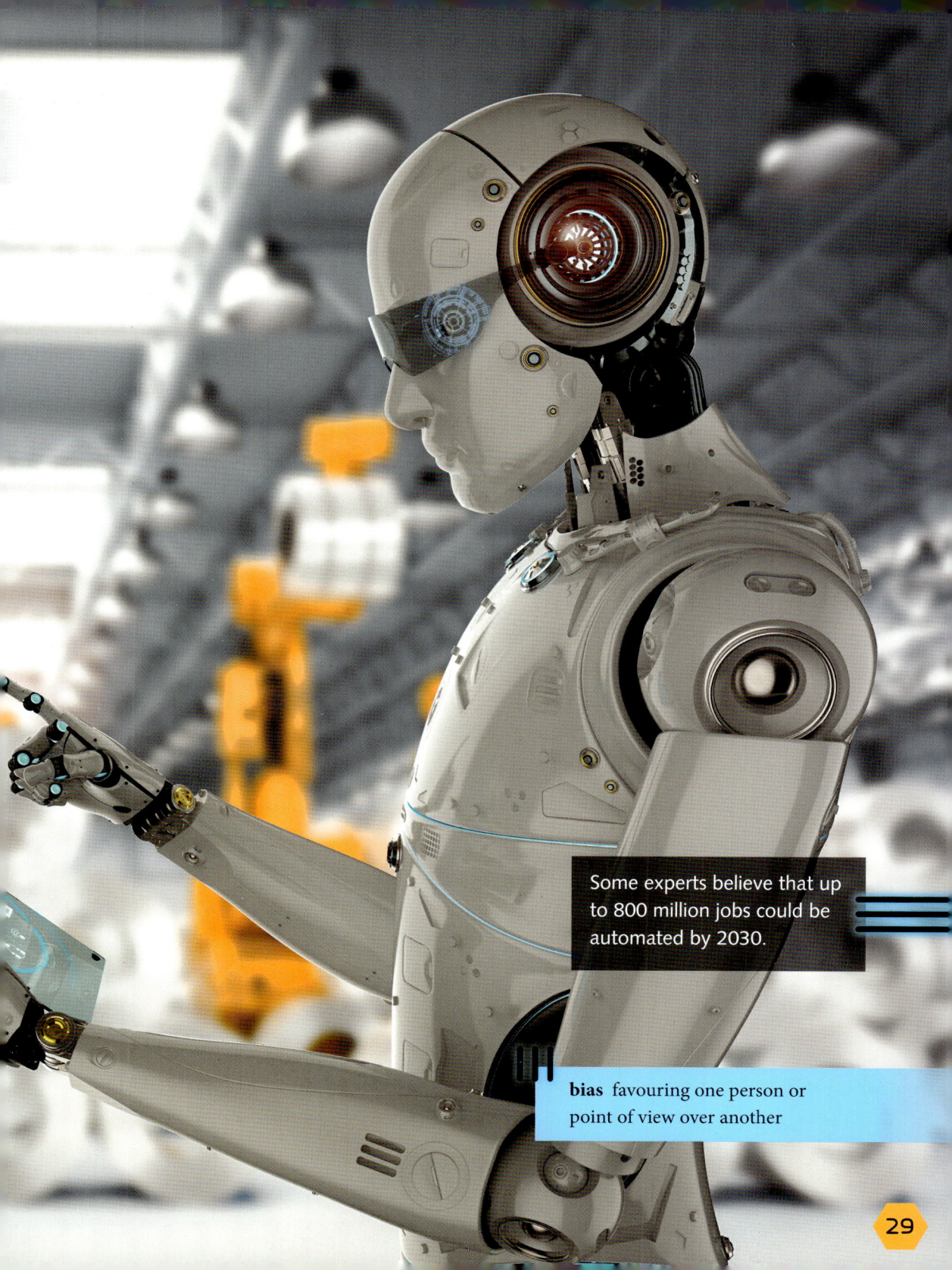

Some experts believe that up to 800 million jobs could be automated by 2030.

bias favouring one person or point of view over another

GLOSSARY

analyse examine something carefully in order to understand it

autonomous able to carry out a job on one's own

bias favouring one person or point of view over another

cloud network of remote servers used to process, manage and store data

diagnose find the cause of a problem

disable stop

drone remote-controlled aircraft or missile that does not have an on-board pilot

facial recognition computer program that identifies people by the features of their faces

humanoid shaped somewhat like a human

pharmacy place where medications are prepared to fill out prescriptions

predict say what you think will happen in the future

prescription order for medicine from a doctor

radar device that uses radio waves to track the location of objects

sensor instrument that detects physical changes in the environment

template document that you can use as a guide when creating a document of your own

FIND OUT MORE

BOOKS

Agricultural Drones (Drones), Simon Rose (Raintree, 2018)

All About Virtual Reality, Jack Challoner (DK Children, 2017)

Robot: Meet the Machines of the Future, Laura Buller, Clive Gifford and Andrea Mills (DK Children, 2018)

WEBSITES

www.bbc.co.uk/newsround/41037709
Learn more about robots and industry.

www.dkfindout.com/uk/computer-coding/what-is-coding
Find out more about computer coding.

INDEX

algorithms 6, 20
AUDREY 20, 21

bias 28
bomb disposal 22, 23

Cafe X 13
cloud 11
crowd safety 25
C-Turtle 23
customer service 11, 18

drones 24–25

education 12, 14

facial recognition 5
FINDER 20, 21
Flippy 12
food service 5, 12–13

Harpy 11
healthcare 4, 8

job loss 28, 29

Kirobo 26

manufacturing 12, 16
Mars rovers 26
media industry 14
military 22, 24

news bots 14

pharmacies 4
Project Maven 24

retail industry 12, 17, 18–19
Robonaut 2 26
robots 4–5, 12–13, 16, 17, 18, 20, 22, 23, 26, 27

search and rescue 20
space exploration 26
speech recognition 10–11, 28

Valkyrie 26, 27
virtual mirrors 19
virtual teaching assistants 14